The Little F
of

ATTITUDE

CW00371569

PHILLIP DAY

 Credence Publications

The Little Book of Attitude

First published in 2005
by Credence Publications

ISBN 1-904015-19-0

Manufactured in Great Britain and Australia by
Credence Publications
PO Box 3
TONBRIDGE
Kent TN12 9ZY UK
www.credence.org

1st ed.

Table of Contents

Welcome to the World of *You*

Hello, my name is Phillip Day.

Thank you so much for taking the time to read this book.

I am a health researcher, author and international speaker who, for the past twenty years, has been fascinated by our attitudes concerning sickness, health and longevity. In fact, the brief of my company, Credence, runs quite a bit wider than just health issues. We report on agendas that are harmful to the public, and our mission now is based in many countries around the world.

I was excited about doing this book. I made the decision returning from Dublin to Holyhead one day on the hydrofoil. You could gaze back at the roiling wake that marked the passing of this fabulous craft, then turn and survey the waves yet to be billowed. So, a book about journeys perhaps? Plan where you're going, set the compass and enjoy the ride? Notes for a good life, maybe? Avoid the negatives, share in the victories; catch the last bus for Brooklyn in the hope the world might be the poorer for your passing – perhaps even the government?

Of course, no-one taught us Life Management at school, those skills everyone needs to survive and thrive in the 21st century. Nevertheless, some rather mighty minds have turned their faculties to how we can cope daily, what we can do to survive and flourish in spite of what life throws at us. So, welcome to *The Little Book of Attitude*, a frank yet heart-warming review of life's major minefields and what can be done about them. A personal collection of tips and hints, homilies, tests and treats concerning the mysteries of 21st century life, who we are and why we do those darned things we do.

Enjoy!

Phillip

How to Use this Book

Please read this first ☺

This book is not designed to replace qualified medical advice. Patients suffering ill-health are, of course, advised to consult a physician. This book *does* encourage you to be discriminatory in what you do with the advice you receive, and encourages you to take control of your healthcare decisions. Ultimately it is up to each to decide on the course of action most appropriate. And, as usual, the *caveat* is well repeated that doctors are your servants not your masters, an arrangement all too easily forgotten.

This book should not be construed as diagnostic or treatment advice for any individual's particular condition. Information contained herein is provided for educational purposes only. Most of the following sections deal with lifestyle problems. Where a 'dis-ease' is discussed, the body will be presenting *physical* symptoms. For more information concerning these physical or 'mental' conditions, please refer to *The ABC's of Disease*. Credence has other titles which deal more specifically with key conditions and subjects relating to health. These are summarised under **Other Disorders** at the end of this book.

Dare to Dream

All creatures desire a good life. A dog snoring by a log fire or tucking into ten pounds of wildebeest is having an Oprah moment compared with sledge-hauling or guard-duty. Ask your friends what a good life might mean to them and you will get the usual lottery wins, sex, rose gardens, big houses, bingo, early retirement, peace of mind and health - indeed, everything the ad industry makes money selling to us.

The basis of a good life is hotly debated in the tabloids and lifestyle magazines. Lottery lout Michael Carroll won £9.7 million at the age of 20 and spends most of his time banger-racing around his home in Swaffham, Norfolk, driving his neighbours batty. For others, the good life means being happy, not having to worry. Still others mark a good life as achievement, satisfaction and emotional wellbeing.

The behavioural experts largely agree that a good life contains more pleasure than pain, where our basic needs are catered for, with a little left over. What about goals? Is a good life one in which our goals are achieved, or is life grander when we don't have to bother? Notice the host of variables the discussion throws up. One person's pain is another's pleasure. I don't like parachuting personally, but thousands live for it. Madonna's basic needs are a little different from Father Alphonso's. Some like it hot. Some like it cold. Some like a lot left over.

Goal!
The good life, which everyone seems to want, means different things to different people. So what do we want?

What do I hope to achieve by the end of the year?
Where would I like to be in five years?
Where in ten years?
After my life is over, how would I like to be remembered?

Goal-setting is a wearisome idea for most, because although we all dream, we understandably fear failure or falling short of the mark, which is why most of us won't do the exercise. Have a go. Answers to the above might variously run:

I wish to be married by the end of the year.
I wish to have a child within five years.
Two by ten.
I wish to be remembered as a good mum.

By the end of the year, I want to be running my own business.
Within five years I want to go international.
In ten years I wish to retire.
I want to be remembered for being fair, hale and hearty.

What do I hope to achieve by the end of the year? *Nothing.*
Where would I like to be in five years? *Sod off.*
Where in ten years? *None of your beeswax.*
How would I like to be remembered? *Who gives a monkey's?*

What are your answers?

Be Inspired!

Making a conscious decision about where you are going is a fundamental necessity for all journeys, even if your desire is to drift where life takes you. Depression is an inability to take action. Often no goals have been set leaving us wandering aimlessly, wondering at the point of it all.

So you want to go to university. To study what? What do you want to achieve with your anthropology degree? You want to be a professional footballer? Write it down. You want to open your own hairdressing salon? Go to next year's concert at Glastonbury? Write a book? Gape at the pyramids of Giza or the Grand Canyon? Get busy scratching pen to paper. You have to want your goals. Heck, you have to dream of them. What do you dream of?

You have no idea?!!

Lighting the Fire

Neither did I in my early twenties, having been through one of the best educational systems in the world – not a clue. So I decided to browse. If I found myself wandering around with time on my hands, I'd visit a bookshop like Barnes and Noble or Waterstones and trawl through the goodies for an hour well spent. I'd look at all the covers and displays and enter a world of achievement, infamy, trial and endeavour. If it's ever been thought about, fought over, conquered or built, someone's done a book on it: Running a business, cooking, the military, space exploration, football, embroidery, love stories, crime, working with animals.

The Start of The Mission

One day in a bookstore in Santa Monica, California, I picked up *World Without Cancer* by G Edward Griffin and read the back of it. Ed's book is about how to treat cancer using food factors, not damaging radiation, surgery or chemotherapy. My family has lost many loved ones to cancer, so I took the book home and became

7

thoroughly inspired by both Ed and his work. My two thoughts at the time? Why on earth is a book like this sitting on Main Street when hundreds of thousands are suffering and dying from this disease? Why am I not seeing any of this on the Six O'Clock News?

Why indeed.
I read why and felt pain.
I got angry.

And you know me, I proceeded to buy up every book I could on cancer and what to do about it and within a year was visiting clinics, speaking to doctors, drafting my own overview book on the subject, *Cancer: Why We're Still Dying to Know the Truth*. But even that wasn't enough. Who was going to publish such a controversial tome? What if my book stayed on the shelves like the one I found of Ed's, even if I did succeed in finding a publisher? (Ha!)

I could have baulked and forgotten the whole thing, and over the next few weeks I nearly did. Then I received word a relative of mine was getting 'the best cancer treatment' and she died anyway, and that only made me the madder. I thought, 'Publishing a book is only about printing it, right? And the world is full of printers. Getting people to read a book is only about telling them the good news and them buying it, so why don't I go out there and just tell them? Why don't I start my own publishing company?'

So I did. I took action. I had the full answer to the cancer problem, backed up by some of the world's most respected experts. As the behavioral gurus declaimed, I had 'obtained control over my sense of certainty' and 'gained leverage'. Today,

Credence books are sold all over the world, have been translated into different languages, and the emails of success continue to pour in from those who have benefited.

Dreamweavers

In this tale we see all the ingredients of taking action and moving forward. Although giving birth to Credence was like dropping a hippo, it seemed effortless at the time *because it was my dream*. A project or career begins with a dream. Sometimes that dream is born out of pain which forces our focus. At the time of writing I have written twelve books, some full length, some pocket guides, each project born of a *dream, a necessity, a desire and compulsion* that what I had to say, the world desperately needed to know about.

Arrogance? Perhaps. Conceit? Definitely. But the desire for action birthed a commitment *that was important to me*, and so my mission was born.

Conviction

Richard Branson is a man who knows how to dream big. From humble beginnings running his record shop out of a London phone box (the only one that worked) to today's globe-trotting mogul owning everything from airlines to insurance, Richard exemplifies the desire to dream big and take action when conviction becomes irresistible. The Dream Business involves everything in the encompassment of the dreamer, on whatever scale the dreaming is done. Often dreamweavers inspire others to action by their example, it's a definable energy, the spark of endeavour, and it lights up the countryside for miles around. Many people no doubt told Richard he would fail.

Dreamkillers

Dreamkillers project their own doubts and failures onto others, and all dreamweavers have a school of them cluttering their wake taking nibbles like remorae on a big fish. The worst dreamkillers are often well-intentioned family members or friends who don't want you to fail. When the dreams become reality, the dreamkillers then discuss how soon your project will crash and burn, as it may have once done with them, which is why they have failed ever since to muster the courage to dream further. Take impartial advice. Avoid advice from dreamkillers.

Uncontainable

Dreamweavers cannot help but try to turn their dreams into reality. Writers cannot help writing. Artists cannot help creating. Nurses cannot help serving. Politicians cannot help blowing hot air. We're too busy, so there is no depression if the dream inspires us. We have a goal. It's our engine, it's what drives us, our passion, motivation, the drop-down, drag-out desire to move from where we are now to where we can be in the future.

Notice the scale does not matter. Organising a village fête or boot sale. Getting married. Rowing up the Amazon. Organising Live 8. Hitler polished off a box of chocolates and invaded Russia (wish he'd stuck to the painting). There are dreamers who only dream, then there are the Big Fish who dominate their dream, refine it, interrogate it, nurture and nourish it; shepherd it onward to its restless, uncontainable fulfilment. Take care what you dream for, you may get it.

Compulsion - Taking the Plunge

For many, the dream may remain just that – a dream. But for the Big Fish, the dream becomes uncomfortable, restless, larger than life, the very imagining of it sparking the desire to dare the project further. A defining moment comes when we take the dream from an idea and do something about it.

Some make this a conscious step and take the decision clearly and soberly. I don't. I dream a book, then I doodle and map out the baby steps. It's only a piece of paper. It's only a computer file. I don't feel committed. But the moment pen hits paper or my fingers the keyboard, I pass through a threshold moment. I go from dreaming to doodling in the blink of an eye. The decision to bring the project out of the dream realm and set it to action has been taken. I am propelled forward as if by an unseen hand. I can bail at any time so I don't feel threatened. But not to doodle is not to know. Know if I can do it.

Looking back, I took the plunge for all my projects in a state of relaxation. I did take advice, but the final decision was mine alone. I'd be on holiday somewhere, lounging in the sun, swishing my leg in the pool. Then I'd get up and order a drink at the Coco Bar, pull out a piece of paper and sit down and doodle. In reality, I am 'gaining leverage'. I am driven by the unseen hand to wonder 'what if?'. I'm not making a decision but I am. I can back out at any time but I won't. Each baby step leads to the next. At each level I am driven by the pleasure of the dream. I dare the project further.

Baby Steps – The Planning Stage

Failure happens. To minimize failure, I test the dream-ladder at every step and take advice. If it passes, it's on to the next rung. If any step fails to lead me to the next, it might need caressing, nourishing, exploring, to see what the block is. If the problem cannot be overcome, I have the option to bail. Sometimes

11

I do, sometimes I don't. I'm not expending valuable resources if the dream does not haul me forward with the irresistible momentum of a freight train. *The dream must impress me immensely or it isn't a dream.*

Learn More About Yourself:
What do you dream about?
What are your passions?
What do you like doing?
Which dreams of yours are restless to be born?
How will you feel if you succeed?
Do you have a box of chocolates and thirty armoured divisions?

Now Ask Yourself:
What do I hope to accomplish by bed-time tonight?
Where do I want to be by the end of the month?
The end of the year?
Where would I like to be in five years?
Where in ten?
After my life is over, how would I like to be remembered?
If I could do anything in the world *right now*, what would it be?
How do I feel about all this?

Only You –
...know what motivates you. As a dreamweaver you can add purpose and context to your life. No goals equals no context to your existence, which can provoke the helpless, 'What's the point of it all?' Big Fish never fall victim. You dared the dream. The dream gives you pleasure. The project is responsible and worthy. It sparked you up in the first place, remember?

What Have I Learned?

I must not fear to dream. It is only dreaming

Dreams I enjoy bring me pleasure

I will dwell on the dreams I am passionate about

I can choose what I want out of life from my desires (the scale does not matter)

What talents do I have which I really enjoy using?

What really motivates me?

Am I restless to achieve what motivates me?

Will my desires and goals bring meaning to my life?

Am I restless to get started?

Pain and Pleasure – Taking Action

One of the great blocks to success is the inability to take action. Once again, the scale of the action does not matter. Taking action is simply the ability to move. Notice how pain motivates. So does pleasure – the carrot and the stick. We can tolerate a certain discomfort, but when it is pain, we take action to do something about it. *We change our state.*

World-famous life coach Anthony Robbins describes survival as the single-most dominant human dynamic. The brain is constantly seeking to avoid pain and gain pleasure, by which we survive. We do those things which bring pleasure, we avoid those things which cause pain – we survive. Both stimuli create action, depending on their intensity. Humans have the unique ability to reassign what causes us pain or pleasure. Robbins is right.[1]

Pain

Pain for most people hurts, which is why Nike's 'Just Do It!', for most people, didn't. 'No pain, no gain' discovered instead a world full of fat people paying £50 a month for a gym membership they never showed up for. We avoid things or people that cause us pain. We aggregate pleasure. Linked with pain is the need *to do something about it.*

Pleasure

...too can provoke action if we let it. Multi-billion-dollar industries have grown up around the need to stop pain or ease it with pleasure. Advertising doyens play pain and pleasure games

---

[1] **Robbins, Anthony** *Awaken the Giant Within*, www.anthonyrobbins.com

like the pros they are. Five hours a night of TV entrainment, infomercials, ads and soaps plug us into the pain matrix. *Pleasure,* the billboards snarl, *You're Not Getting Any.* Cooking gurus make food we can't get at. Exotic travel shows contrast dream locations with our own crummy neighbourhoods. Adverts show people in pain gaining pleasure from the advertiser's product. We want those things we are told will bring us pleasure: cars, sofas, quad bikes, fashion clothes, Crazy Frog ring-tones and, if there's cash left over, a card for the spouse.

Placebo/Nocebo
Faith Changes Your Biochemistry

Pain and pleasure affect us at such a fundamental level, our thoughts change our biochemistry. Witness someone caught in a traffic jam who has to be somewhere in a hurry. Someone in love. The fight or flight response when danger threatens. There are four interesting effects that spin off from this:

Threat = mental pain = depressed immunity
No-threat = mental pleasure = raised immunity
Placebo = raised immunity
Nocebo = depressed immunity

Someone given a fake pill or placebo[2], *who holds to be true* that the pill will heal them, stands a good chance of recovering by boosting their immunity. If they know the pill is a fake, however, any benefit is lost and the effect does not work. There's faith for you.

---

[2] **placebo** – a harmless, pharmacologically inactive medicine given to a patient which effects 'a cure'.

For centuries, doctors used placebo to assist in their work. Drugs are tested today in double-blind, placebo-controlled studies to see whether the drug can outperform the placebo effect.[3] Witness two doctor's declarations almost 100 years apart:

"I was brought up, as I suppose every physician is, to use placebo, bread pills, water injections and other devices –. I used to give them by the bushels –"
Professor Richard Cabot, Harvard Medical School, 1903

"Whatever the rights and wrongs, placebo prescribing is widely practised and, if we admit it to ourselves, <u>so is the habit of prescribing for largely social reasons</u>." [emphasis *moi*]
Dr K Palmer, British general practitioner, 1998

Nocebos have the opposite effect to placebos and depress immunity. Nocebos don't have to be 'bad' pills at all. They can be anything we process in a negative fashion. Consider the following:

A son told repeatedly, 'You're no bloody good.' – Nocebo
'Good news, Mrs H, the cancer is gone.' – Placebo
A patient told, 'You have three months to live.' – Nocebo
Bad news – Nocebo
Good news – Placebo
Love – Placebo
Hate - Nocebo

Changing State
When we avoid pain and move towards pleasure, we 'change our state'. Media teaches us how to handle the spasms of life

---

3 Studies conducted where neither the patient nor doctor knows whether the tested substance is the real drug or placebo

variously with beer, football, cigarettes, sex, drugs, violence and lots of chocolate. For the young, bad news nocebos, financial woes, stressed relationships and late nights at the office are countered with *perceived* placebic effects such as shopping, food, clubbing, sex, alcohol and controlled substances which change mental focus to ban pain and gain pleasure. We like how pleasure feels. It's feral. 'Just Do It!', so we bloody did, mate.

The older relieve stress with more sedate placebic actions: reading a book, going to the pub, watching a good film, having friends around. There is nothing wrong with changing state, so long as the effects do not harm us or others. Sometimes though, we banish symptoms instead of the cause: the headache treated with painkillers; money problems with shopping; a gnarly husband with Valium. In the meantime, the underlying problem continues unabated.

Learn More About Yourself
- What causes you pain?
- What causes you pleasure?
- What placebic events are operating in your life?
- Which nocebos?
- How do you change your state to relax?
- Are any of these state-changes harming you?
- Are you solving your problems or just masking the symptoms?

What You Can Do
- If I am unhappy with my life, I can do something about it
- I can take action
- I will only take action if I am uncomfortable enough

- When I am uncomfortable or motivated enough, I gain leverage
- Gaining leverage is when I am compelled to act *immediately* and *irresistibly*
- To take action I must decide where I want to go
- Setting goals gives me a course of action
- Now I can plan the steps to carry out my mission
- Each step must impress me enough to move on to the next
- My goals must be irresistible, impress the heck out of me
- I must take action if I want a result
- To achieve my goals, *I must really want them*
- I can improve my well-being by increasing placebic effects in my life and decreasing nocebos
- I can steer my own destiny
- I can really do this

Pavlov's Dog - Brain-Patterning
A brief guide to neuro-associative programming

Take a Jack Russell and throw it a stick. The dog charges after the stick and brings it back. You reward the dog with a biscuit. Now the dog's brain is thinking, 'Stick. Biscuit, Biscuit. Stick. Stick. Biscuit' and links pleasure to it. Stick-getting is thus to the dog a placebic event. Next time you throw the stick, the dog is thinking 'biscuit'. You now have Pavlov's Dog.

Notice the dog's brain also records everything else in the three dimensional arena about it, children shrieking, church bells, horn toots, the ice-cream van jingle, and links pleasure to them. If the stick-throwing is repeated often enough (usually over 15 – 30 days), these are grouped together in the animal's mind under 'Stick-Getting' *and can trigger each other*. Both pain and pleasure result from this type of associative brain-patterning. The habit is formed:

- Eagles songs remind of California = sun, sea and sex = pleasure
- Relaxation reminds of cigarettes = changing state = pleasure
- A woman's perfume reminds of Mother = pleasure
- Spiders = the movie, *Arachnophobia* = spiders killing humans = survival threat = pain
- Public speaking = failing in public = pain
- Exercise = pain
- Play = pleasure

Advertisers rely on Pavlov's Dog to link beer with football, aftershave with the FA Cup, make-up with Miss World, seduction with Ibiza, to create associative pleasure in the recipient. The technique is known as neuro-associative conditioning. Ad time sells big time during major sporting events due to the power of its association. Millions watching America's Superbowl are in a receptive state of pleasure, they are ripe for a linking, and so are you, sunshine. Consider how advertising shapes our behaviour with associative conditioning, resulting in the lure of a positive state-change:

- Money problems (pain) = Re-mortgaging advert = removal of the survival threat (pain) = Loan = pleasure. *State-change*
- Lack of love life (pain) = Aftershave/perfume advert = gained attention = Girlfriend/boyfriend = pleasure. *State-change*
- Dirty kitchen (pain) = cleaning product advert = squeaky clean kitchen = pleasure. *State-change*

The advertising industry highlights problems and offers solutions, usually the ad client's product or service. Notice the perceived state-change to pleasure in the recipient. Neuro-associative conditioning is so potent it underwrites the holiday, auto, housing, insurance, advertising, marketing and public relations industries, to name but a few. Aye, lass, big business.

The Hegelian Dialectic

Politicians are at it too, linking pain to events to gain power to change things. The Hegelian Dialectic involves a three-step process that justifies solutions which result in an expansion of government and the tax-load. Populations can be educated into accepting laws and restrictions they normally wouldn't if it means the removal of a survival threat (pain).

- Real or imagined problems in society are raised and pain is linked to them (*the thesis*). Iraq, Afghanistan, global warming, immigration, crime, etc.
- The media provokes a widespread *emotional* response to the problem, which it reports and agonises over in excruciating detail (more pain - the reaction or *antithesis*)
- Finally, after everyone has exhausted the gin-bottle and Prozac worrying about the survival threat, the public begs politicians to take action (*the synthesis*)

Social Control

Take ten monkeys and put them in a cage. Dangle a banana from the roof of the cage. Place a step-ladder under the banana. If any monkey approaches the ladder, hose down the entire group with a powerful jet of water. Soon, when the monkeys begin to connect the banana to the violent hosing, they will begin enforcing the 'no-banana' rule on their own, by beating any monkey who comes near the ladder, in order to spare themselves another hosing.

With the group now collectively enforcing the 'no-banana' rule and the fire hose no longer needed to keep the monkeys away from the ladder, take one of the monkeys out of the cage and introduce a newcomer. Of course, this newcomer will be curious about the banana and will probably try to climb the ladder, but the other nine monkeys will beat him senseless if he even tries, so he finally gives up. Once the newcomer has adjusted to the 'no-banana' rule, remove another of the original monkeys and introduce another newcomer. Repeat until all the original monkeys have been replaced by newcomers, none of whom has ever actually seen the fire hose, much less been sprayed with it.

What we have, in the end, is a cage full of monkeys conditioned to enforce the 'no-banana' rule on each other, though none even knows why. Ultimately the reason why they are enforcing the 'no-banana' rule is because that's the way it's always been done, the illogical reason driving this adopted behaviour lost in the mists of time.

(No primates were harmed in
the imagining of this experiment).

Spin

...is neuro-associative conditioning. It *reassigns* pain or pleasure to change our focus. Everyone's guilty of it. Some of the effects are local, others can be far-reaching, even catastrophic.

Potential global flu epidemic = 750,000 might die = perceived survival threat = pain = new vaccine = get vaccinated to remove the survival threat = relief = pleasure. Result: *State-change*

Saddam Hussein = The Beast = 45-minute warning of deployment of WMDs = perceived survival threat = pain = go to war to remove the survival threat = relief = pleasure. Result: *State-change*

Vitamin pills can harm you = perceived survival threat = pain = propose new legislation to restrict access to supplements = political action is taken to remove the survival threat = relief = pleasure. Result: *State-change*

What we link pain and pleasure to constructs our world-view and our likes and dislikes. It's an amazing tool for good. It's an amazing tool for mischief too:

'There are many potential epidemics' = millions will die = survival threat = take action and get vaccinated for everything = removal of the survival threat

'Saddam Hussein' = survival threat = Middle Eastern = all Middle Easterners are potential survival threats = take action to avoid Middle-Easterners = removal of the survival threat

'Vitamin pills can harm you' = nutritional medicine can be a survival threat = take action and stay with the experts and their drugs = removal of the survival threat

Reassigning Pain and Pleasure

Humans have the ability to reassign pain and pleasure, thereby changing our focus, behaviour and world-view. Once again, the results can be placebic or nocebic. By all means choose the motivation which suits you best, I won't tell:

Exercise = pain. Play = pleasure. What if by playing I exercise? Result: Exercise = pleasure

Gym = male pain. Girls wearing next to nothing = male pleasure. Watching girls working out wearing next to nothing = male pleasure. Result: Gym = male pleasur

Gym = female pain. That girl with the worked-out body is getting looked at = female pain = if I have such a body I will get looked at = female pleasure. Result: Gym = female pleasure

Gym = pain. Obesity = pain. Working out will remove fat = pleasure. Result: Gym = pleasure

Gym = pain. Heart condition = pain. Exercise and diet under supervision may remove the survival threat. Result: Gym = pleasure

Etc, etc, etc.

Learn More About Yourself

The reassigning of pain and pleasure is fundamental to changing behaviour. Try this exercise:

1. Take a piece of paper and draw a line down the middle
2. In the left-hand column, write down all the things about yourself you would like to change or be rid of
3. In the right-hand column, write down all the things you would like to become
4. Link pain to those things you wish to lose. Link pleasure to those things you wish to gain. Conduct repeatedly in a state of emotion daily for thirty days
5. As you do, reconfirm by reverse motivation, which means linking pleasure to the result of getting rid of the 'Outs'. Then link pain to not gaining the 'Ins'

Here are some examples:

Outs	*Ins*
Quit smoking	Must exercise
Quit nail-biting	Must learn French
Quit being angry	Must laugh more
Quit worrying	Must eat better
Quit fearing death	Must take a holiday
Quit overspending	Must forgive/be kinder

Reassign as follows:

To get rid of the Outs – **Link massive pain and repeat in a state of emotion consistently over thirty days:**
Quit smoking: Deliver big pain whenever the desire to smoke
Quit nail-biting: Deliver big pain whenever the desire to nibble
Quit being angry: Deliver big pain whenever the desire to fury
Quit worrying: Link big pain to the act of worrying
Quit fearing death: Like big pain to the act of fearing death
Quit overspending: Link big pain to being in debt

Now reverse motivate: **Link massive pleasure and repeat in a state of emotion consistently over thirty days:**
Quit smoking: Imagine pleasure at not smoking
Quit nail-biting: Imagine pleasure at having nice nails
Quit being angry: Imagine pleasure at not having a heart attack
Quit worrying: Imagine how great it will feel not to be depressed
Quit fearing death: Experience pleasure at developing a belief system to explain the unknown
Quit overspending: Imagine the pleasure of not having to worry about money

To gain the Ins – **Link massive pleasure and repeat in a state of emotion consistently over thirty days:**
Must exercise: Link big pleasure to 'playing'
Must learn French: Go to Paris and enjoy (take lots of money)
Must laugh more: Get out with friends and have a blast
Must eat better: Imagine how good I will look and feel
Must take a holiday: You're right, I deserve one
Must forgive/be kinder: Bring great pleasure to others

Ins – **Reverse Motivation: Link massive pain and repeat in a state of emotion consistently over thirty days:**
Must exercise: Link big pain to being unhealthy
Must learn French: Link big pain to not being able to communicate
Must laugh more: Link big pain to being grumpy
Must eat better: Link big pain to unsightly/unhealthy overweight (survival threat)

25

Experience Success

Nothing succeeds like success. Success is the mother of all placebos, it tells us we are on the right track. Success is gained with each rung of the ladder; a measurable drop in weight; gazing at your new company's letterhead; a trip to Venice; winning a tournament; the birth of a child; a new house; a pay-raise; a finished book; peace. Track your progress. Enjoy your successes.

The above patterns should be reinforced constantly over thirty days, then several times a week for the next sixty. The brain will learn any new patterning if the conditioning is repeated in a state of emotion *consistently*.

Guarding Input
Pitching the odds in your favour
*Tell a lie, loud enough, long enough and often enough,
and the people will believe it.'* (Adolf Hitler)

It's a jungle out there.

What we focus on becomes our reality.

What's going on in Equador?

Who cares? I'm not focused on Equador.

What am I focused on?

And what is it doing to me?

'One study involving more than 700 families found that 14-year-old boys who watched relatively more television were more likely to have assaulted or committed a serious act of aggression against someone by the time they were 22 years old. A similar pattern was found among females, but the relationship was much weaker.

Another study found that violence in the media can have a profound effect on the behaviour of children and teens and that TV violence is associated with aggression among children as young as 4 years.

Preschoolers who watch television violence and play violent video games are more likely to show high levels of aggression and antisocial behaviour than those not exposed, according to another study.'[4]

Yet another example of neuro-associative conditioning. TV can work for good. Mostly it works for our undoing.

Input
... is everything we allow to enter us.
What we consume
What we see
What we hear
What we experience
What we touch
What we smell

Output
...is our reaction to the above: our deeds, thoughts, patterning and emotions.

The more positive the input (placebo), the more positive the output, the more positive the patterns, the more positive the performance. And, of course, the reverse is true (nocebo).

The Danger of Media
Media includes advertising, news and entertainment. Media is input and changes the way we interpret the world. Media chooses what we see. Constant repetitions override and re-write opinions and patterning. Media is neuro-associative conditioning on steroids. It can be a force for good. Then again, through selective reporting, all Roman Catholic priests can become paedophiles. All

---

4 www.mercola.com

dark-featured, moustachioed Middle-Easterners can become terrorists. All felons in Los Angeles are 5' 10", 160 lb black males in their early twenties not wearing a shirt. You get the picture.

Televised imagery affects real-world behaviour, the ad industry depends on it. The brain on a sub-conscious level cannot distinguish between what it experiences and what it is shown. Bad news brings pain. Good news brings pleasure. The Six O'Clock News is almost all bad news, which means The Six O'Clock News = pain/nocebo. Most of what is covered is none of our business and does not affect us directly, yet we subconsciously take on the pain.

How does a constant tide of bad news
affect the way you view the world?

Constantly misrepresenting the scale of a threat keeps the populace in a state of mental siege. Relentless coverage throws the spooks into everyone. Consider:

"To get the nation healthier we must have more vaccinations, more hospitals, more doctors and nurses, more drugs, more donations for more research, and higher taxes. If we don't, continued disease poses a survival threat."

A lie repeated loud enough, long enough and often enough is still a lie. Professor Chris Bulstrode, US orthopaedic surgeon turned medical lecturer, is not the only member of his profession to make the case for *less* doctors for better health, not more:

"More doctors just means more illness. If we want a healthier and happier country, we should get rid of a lot of doctors. I

cannot have been the only person who was absolutely incensed to discover that when the Berlin Wall came down, the military strength of the Eastern Block was an order of magnitude less than we had been led to believe. I want to try all the Western generals for lying to the public about how strong the Russians were. These generals have done three things over the last thirty years. They have frightened the hell out of the Russians, they have frightened the hell out of us, and they have stolen a huge amount of money from the budget that could have been used elsewhere. As I was thinking about this, I realized that this is exactly what we as doctors do in healthcare."

Heavy on Our Heart

TV has a strong 'conforming' effect on us, even if we think it doesn't. One in five under-fifteens in Britain is obese. Obesity in America causes 300,000 deaths a year with the total healthcare costs for overweight amounting to a hefty *$100 billion*. 7.3% of Americans officially have diabetes, amounting to more than 10% of the population if the undiagnosed cases are considered.[5] If one totals the number of American citizens weighing between 10 – 30lbs over their average weight for height, 65% of the population falls into that category.

So, what do we see advertised on American TV every night? Junk food, slurpies, pizza, chocolate - constant repetition installs the pattern to choose the food we're told will bring the greatest pleasure.

Consider by the time a child is 16, he will have seen 300,000 acts of gratuitous violence, torture, mutilation, suicide and

---

[5] www.mercola.com

murder on television, at the cinema, and now on his PC. The Comedy Channel has us laughing at euthanasia, adultery, religion and death in a way that makes it all funnier than hell. Hollywood taught us how to enjoy the 'buzz' of sin without the aggravation of accountability in much the same way Ray Kroc showed us how to scoff a Big Mac without the aggravation of the abattoir.

What a Turn-On

Media distorts our world-view with excessive focus on events _we have never personally experienced_. Newspapers gather up all the bad news around the world and dump it on our breakfast table. Terrorism. Disasters. Live sex acts occur in Mediterranean nightclubs, young female holidaymakers taking part while their admiring mothers look on. Drunken brawls in city streets. News of abuses of the young. The killing of little children by other little children. A British father rapes his own daughter then murders her. What was once unthinkable seems to have become commonplace. Or has it?

Dysfunctional input can help society fulfil the prophecy it constantly witnesses on TV. In 1976, the number of reported child abuse cases in America was 670,000. By the early 90s, this figure had risen to nearly 3 million. Movies, soaps, teen magazines and social-climber periodicals across the world deify sex, promiscuity, adultery and drunkenness. Drug abuse is now so widespread in the world's conurbations that when London's Metropolitan Police randomly searched a large cross-section of club-goers in the King's Cross area in 1998, 100% of them were found to be carrying, or under the influence of 'controlled' drugs.

Upwards of 25% of the videos rented in the US each year are pornographic. One Pentagon telephone audit showed $300,000 of taxpayers' money had been spent on 1(900) sex lines. At the last count, within a few blocks of the Department of Justice in Washington DC, there were 37 'adult' bookstores, 8 X-rated theatres and 15 topless bars. No pain, apparently, in the world's superpower capital.

The Double Mind

British TV today is a smorgasbord of Big Brother ogling, Celebrity Love Island shenanigans, the hate-filled faces of soap opera, Sex and the City, an autopsy performed live for a Kentucky-Fried-Chicken-munching public. We desire pleasure no matter the consequences, happily divorcing cause from effect, what everything is doing to us.

Thus arises the double mind, a society able to moralise in the newspapers about rape, murder and sex abuse, while having no problem accommodating the latest *Kill Bill* movie advertised on the very next page. England wept like babies during the serial run of the program *Hearts of Gold*, seeing ordinary folk doing good deeds for one another, dissolving the nation into sentimental goo. But the following day it was 'Hearts of Lead' as we cussed out the kids, gobbled down the porridge and carved up the grannies on our mad dash into work.

There's one thing at which we [Britain] DO lead the world. And we should hang our heads in shame: Britain has the highest rate of unmarried teenage mothers - nine times worse than Japan. Why is Britain so different? Not because we don't teach children about contraception. Just the opposite – <u>we teach them too much and in the wrong way</u>.

The more sexually aware our children become at too early an age, the more they are tempted. Tragically, it has become unfashionable to drum into children the word 'No'. We are paying the price in wrecked lives. [6]

This from *The Sun*, page 8. Turn five pages back and drool at the daily half-page photograph of a teenage girl stripped to the saddle in provocative pose, earning some pin-money as she breaks onto the 'modelling' scene. Is *The Sun* doing its bit to prevent our youth from being sexually 'tempted'? Hardly. But such hypocritical rubbish passes us by with nary a blink.

"I want to be famous!" the school children chorus.
"Famous for what?' asks the teacher.
"Just famous!'

The double mind: "A mind profoundly at war with itself and ignorant even of that fact."[7]

The Twenty-Third Channel
The TV is my shepherd,
I shall not want,
It makes me lie down on the sofa,
It leads me away from the fridge,
It destroys my soul,
It leads me in the path of sex and violence
For the sponsor's sake.
Yea, though I walk
In the shadow of social responsibilities,

6 *The Sun*, 15th May 1998
7 **Hoffman, Michael** *Secret Societies and Psychological Warfare*, Wiswell Ruffin House, 1992

There will be no interruption,
For the TV is with me,
Its cable and remote,
They comfort me.
It prepares a commercial for me
In the presence of all my worldliness.
It anoints my head with consumerism,
My coveting runneth over.
Surely laziness and ignorance
Shall follow me
All the days of my life.
And I shall dwell in the house
Watching TV forever.

Learn More About Yourself

What sort of input am I willingly subscribing to?
What effect can I see this having on me?
Is the double mind in evidence in my life?
How do I reconcile my hypocrisies?
Does this bother me?
Has media usurped my right to make up my mind based on my own experience, or am I *given* my opinions?
Do I think media is a force for good?
Do I think media is a force for ill?
And the question they'll take you out and shoot you for asking:

DO I REALLY NEED MEDIA AT ALL?

Based on your answers, try switching off the TV for fourteen days. If you break out in a sweat and can't, at least total up the time you spend in front of the box, reading newspapers, listening to the radio, etc., and consider what you could have done with the time instead:

- Played some sport and made myself healthier
- Got a university degree
- Started a business
- Written a good book
- Read a good book
- Organised worthwhile activities for my children
- Saved the £40-a-month cable fee and put it towards a college education for my child instead
- Created something
- Served someone

Moral of the story?

Pain in, pain out.

Pleasure in, pleasure out.

Guard your input like a pit-bull.

Practise good thoughts (I'm not sure pit-bulls do this).

One Day at a Time

I am a big fan of imagining each day as a life. Mine. It has a beginning, a middle and an end. I do the following for each new day:

I wake up (always a good idea)
I lie in bed and contemplate my day ahead
I ask: What do I wish to accomplish by bed-time tonight?
How will I feel if I succeed?
Are some of these things what I personally want?
Does the day I am planning impress the heck out of me?

Today, I will not worry about the G8 summit, a Martian invasion, suicide bombs in Baghdad, Third World hunger, an asteroid striking the earth, or what David Beckham wore to the Met Bar last night (all nocebos). Today I will leave the TV off, the newspaper in the corner store, the radio silent, and clean up my input. I can be the architect of this new day which has been given to me. I intend to raise my standards and live it well.

The Possibilities Are Endless
I will write the first page of my new book. Just one page
I will speak to one person who thinks I've forgotten them
I will practise what I am good at
I will dominate my day and carefully steer it
I will simplify, simplify, simplify
I will guard what comes out of my mouth
I will do no harm to myself or others
I will eat food that will nourish me
I will relish freedom unchained from negative input

Repetition in a state of emotion forms the attitude pattern. Every day I do this makes the following day easier. Six days of accomplishment means a *whole* week I lived well. So much done in one week! Negative input was out. All the positives in. I ate simple, fresh, nutritious food. I drank clean water. I breathed. I did not watch the Simpsons.

Hmmm. Breathe.

Feels good to breathe.

On the seventh day, I rest.

Play.

I break the cycle.

Every day, I *agree* to enjoy at least one overwhelming, optimistic experience (placebo). Each day is planned around this event. If all else fails and the Martians invade, I am still determined to enjoy this event. Today, Samantha and I will take Rosie for a walk in the forest. The dog's tail drums in anticipation. I know things about labradors. They are not worried about their bank manager or a Sarin gas attack on the Bakerloo Line. It's about rabbits chased, sticks cracked in jaws, the swim in the pond and aroma plethora. Sheer pleasure derived from endeavour. And the dinner. The dinner. Oh, the dinner –

Where You Live

Furnish a home environment to reflect peace and optimism (placebo). *Agree* to make good choices. Hang pictures you adore. Play music that soothes. Have just one clock in the house.

Invite plants and flowers to participate. If you have a garden, grow things there. If I walk out and stand in ours, I gain a better perspective of my own existence. Bees bumble. Birds warble. Plants grow, live and die, and that is apparently all right with them too.[8]

Cleve Backster, CIA scientist and inventor of the polygraph (lie-detector), spent years recording plants' reactions to humans. No fruitcake Cleve, though some of his peers were unhappy with the proof plants bond with humans, even our pain, Mr Clinton. Welcome to the fascinating world of the Unknowable. How does it work? Haven't a clue. Every day, though, a further secret is revealed if I trouble to search for it. One day I'll know. One day.[9]

Thinks at Sunset

Did my surroundings today reflect optimism and peace? Yes.
Did I succeed in planning my day and accomplishing it? *Yes!*
I commanded my day and carefully steered it
I wrote the first page of my new book
I spoke to one person who believed I had forgotten them
My goals guided my actions
I practised what I was good at
I did no harm to myself or another
I had an overwhelming, optimistic experience
This was the day that was given to me, which I lived well
And the dinner. The dinner. Oh, the dinner –

---

[8] **Tomkins, P and C Bird** *The Secret Life of Plants*, HarperCollins 2002
[9] Ibid.

Facing Your Mountains - Worry

Worriers perfect the art of imagining how things will turn out for the worst. Do not dwell on impromptu evil imaginings. You can't stop the birds flying over your head, but you can stop them nesting in your hair.

The best way over mountains is one rock at a time. The best advice about mountains is to face them. Mountains cause worry. But not if you overcome them.

Be an overcomer.

Was a time we fell off our bike, picked ourselves up, dusted ourselves down and carried on as if nothing had happened. Today, when we fall off our bike, we're dusted off by a social worker, referred into a victim support group, and if that fails, we can sue the government on legal aid. Alternatively, if we're slam-dunked by some appalling stroke of 'fate' such as wanton debt, an illicit affair or a Prozac or Valium dependency, we can slip into the 'victim' jacket and seek out the nearest agony aunt, astrologer or Feng Shui advisor. These are only too happy to oblige with the latest scoop, pocketing our money and reassuring us it's nothing WE did, it's just society's a dog, the new moon's in the 11th house and the furniture's all in the wrong place.

If something about me needs changing, <u>I</u> need to change it
<u>I</u> stopped overcoming
Time for <u>me</u> to overcome

Learn More About Yourself

Divide a sheet of paper vertically down the middle with a line. On the left, write down all the things that worry you which you CAN do something about. On the right, list all the things that worry you which you CANNOT do anything about.

Rank the left-hand column in descending order of bother, i.e. the most worrisome problem at the top. Do the same with the right-hand column of worries you can do nothing about.

- You are now staring at your mountains
- You have an order of worries to tackle, commencing with the most worrying
- Worry caused by the problems you can do something about will diminish ONCE YOU TAKE ACTION
- Imagine each problem resolved and how you will feel about that
- Imagine the relief/pleasure you will gain by overcoming
- Dwell on the peace of mind gained by overcoming
- Imagine the continued pain/anxiety of not overcoming
- List out the steps required to overcome the problem
- How badly do you want to conquer the problem?
- Now take action, focusing repeatedly on the pleasure/relief you gain at every step
- Be consistent and repetitive. If you falter, link further big pain to having to tolerate the worry further

Things You Cannot Do Anything About

Problems beyond our control cause unnecessary worry. There can be no action, since the problem is beyond our capacity to influence, so why worry?

I am going to die one day (perhaps today)

A super-quake will snap California off into the Pacific

An asteroid will strike the earth

The sun will flame out, plunging the earth into darkness

A tsunami will re-engulf Indonesia

My family will perish in a freak accident

I will become a victim of terrorists

- Link big pain to unnecessary worrying
- Link big pleasure to *not unnecessarily worrying*
- Imagine the relief of not having to burden yourself with matters beyond your control. While you cannot fix the whole world, sometimes you *can* fix your little corner of it. Is your worry caused by junk input? You can, of course, take action on a smaller scale, i.e:
- Move out of California
- Don't take your holidays in Jakarta
- Then again, *why worry?*
- Overcoming unnecessary worry is about confronting the worry itself, examining it dispassionately, then deleting it in a state of positive emotion with a change in focus. How about:
- A coward dies a thousand deaths, a brave man dies but one
- I can be brave. *Why worry?*
- Terrorism fails when I fail to be terrorised. *Why worry?*
- Have I actually experienced terrorism?
- Are my worries disproportionate to what actually happens to me?
- Am I reacting reasonably?
- Why don't I restrict input which fosters unnecessary worry?

- Why not give my life meaning and context to explain why I am here?
- If I live my life well, my journey's end will be expected, even welcomed

Attitude Adjustment: The Mental

Reconciling Your Fear of Death

I receive many emails on depression and the fear of death, so let's have a look. The fact is, the death-rate is still one per person with a 100% hit ratio, we're all going to make it. No-one gets out of this gig alive. Every person at some stage will ask the four big questions:

1. Who am I?
2. Where did I come from?
3. What am I doing here?
4. Where am I going when this life is over?

Note these describe a journey with a beginning, a middle and an end. If I add context and purpose to my life, goals can be met and the journey's end, like the close of a day, is expected, even welcomed. If I have no belief system to explain why I am here, I can find myself with no clue to the outcome, no context or value to my life, becoming more desperate as I grow older, not really knowing what it's all been for.

Teaching Despair

There should be a Campaign for Truth in Science. For the past one hundred years, schools have gone to great effort NOT to teach Life Management (the skills required to overcome) but the hopeless theory of evolution. Evolution teaches we are here by blind, random chance; the universe banged into existence from matter the size of a full-stop. Then a speck of dust somehow developed life and consciousness via billions of 'beneficial

43

mutations' (no small potatoes), evolving from simple to complex (in spite of the Second Law of Thermodynamics) into insects, fish, reptiles, birds and finally Eddie Izzard. That Eddie was then able to consider said speck of dust and marvel at his own ancestry (even though no-one saw any of it happen) is another truth-busting paradox that passes us by with nary a blink.

Evolution is sold to the public as science. *What science?*

Today, evolution is taught in classrooms and universities as fact. It is a far cry from fact. If evolution were fact, we'd have to accept it. God and religious arguments aside (which always hound the debate), the theory of evolution is scientific and social fraud on a Herculean scale, and just that, *a theory:*

- BILLIONS of years ago, the Big Bang banged
- MILLIONS of years ago dinosaurs roamed the Earth
- HUNDREDS OF THOUSANDS of years ago, cave men were thumping each other with mallets
- Frogs turned into princes
- Whales into cows
- Dinosaurs into birds
- No-one saw any of it
- No transitional forms have ever been found
- Some think evolution's what happened
- It's a theory, a belief system, a religion impersonating science
- And not good science at all, Prof Richard Dawkins

I Don't Think You're Human

Like most religions, evolution turned deadly. Josef Stalin, Pol Pot, Adolf Hitler and Serb extremists all used evolution to justify their slaughters of 'inferior' populations. Today there's abortion (it's not human yet); black people, aborigines, native Indians, etc. (not as evolved from apes as whites). We have been teaching our kids for the past one hundred years they are nothing but a monkey, so why are we surprised they behave like monkeys? (By the way, why do we still have monkeys if they evolved into humans?)

What's The Big Deal?

- Evolution teaches survival of the fittest
- If you don't get given, you learn to take
- No right or wrong (pesky God concepts)
- No morality inherited (fun-stalling religious rubbish)
- Life, in the long run, is pointless
- You are nothing but a pollywog that crawled out of a mud-swamp BILLIONS of years ago to begin your slow scrape up to Wall Street
- You're just a 'human resource'
- You die and go back to star-dust, none of it meant anything
- Have a nice day ☺

Evolution is rubbish science however much you dislike the idea.[10] In man's restless quest to know the unknowable, we have no choice but to accept what we cannot scientifically prove on faith; in other words, what we think happened. A scientist's guess on where you came from is as good as yours. Whatever we teach our children to explain why they're here, let it fit more of the facts than evolution, and let it instil positive values not hopelessness.

---

[10] For a full *scientific* exposé on the myth of evolution, see: **Sodera, Vij,** *One Small Speck to Man,* www.credence.org

45

That said, if you wish to believe grandpappy was an orang-utan, go ahead, it was a free country when I got up this morning. But don't teach it to our kids as science. And don't teach it in the universities as fact. Coots, next thing they'll be telling us Hillary Clinton is running for president.

'How about not equating death with stopping?' - **A Morissette**

Make your belief-system a cracking one. I am a great believer that life's experiences help you develop one. Actually, reconciling your place in the Grand Plan is less about making a monkey out of you than finding out if there *is* a Grand Plan, a personal mission, one you were born for. Investigate this awesome subject. Be careful. Be interested. Be amazed.

A Good Conscience is a Good Pillow

Thomas à Kempis writes: *'Very soon it will be over with you here; then, see how things stand. Today we are, and tomorrow we are gone. And when we are taken out of sight, we soon pass out of mind. Oh, the dullness and hardness of our hearts that only think of the present and do not look forward more to the future. This being the case, you ought to master yourself in every act and thought as if you were to die today. If you had a good conscience, you would not fear death so much…. If you are not prepared today, how will you be ready tomorrow? …When that final hour does come, you will begin to think quite differently about all your past life, and you will be exceedingly sorry that you were so careless and remiss.'*

Well said. Live life with no regrets. Drag any skeletons out of the closet and bury them under the patio. Forgive those who have wronged you. Ask forgiveness from those you have wronged, even if you do not receive it. Own a good conscience. Always be aware of the context of your life and where you are on the journey. Do you lack purpose? Dream goals that get you excited. Then reinforce them repeatedly in a state of positive emotion.

Live Life to The Full

...need not mean parachuting from the Eiffel Tower, swimming with sharks or bungy-jumping from the Clifton Suspension Bridge. It's about enjoying what you do, always aware of your context and where you are on the journey. Goal-setting daily (*What do I want to accomplish by bed-time tonight?*) is my personal favourite, for each day lived has been thought about in advance. Achieving, on whatever scale, bestows satisfaction. Relaxation and play provide pleasure. A life lived to the full is one where goals have been met and pleasure and play abound with a clear conscience.

- Travel
- See the world
- Ask questions
- What does my photo album have in it?
- Am I smiling or scowling?
- Who knocked the Sphinx's nose off anyway?
- What happens when I press *this* at Cape Canaveral?

There are people near you who will die never having ever really lived. Fear holds them back. Fear to explore what they were told was a dangerous world. Fear they might fail. Fear they might not. One died a moment ago, a life of lost opportunities they probably wished they had taken.

Never Retire

When productivity ends, so can our will to go on. A gold watch and a pat on the back can be interpreted as the golden boot: 'All right, thank you very much. Make way for the young now.' Nothing but a corporate human resource, off to the post office and then to the scrap-heap, drawing your pension once a week and scratching down your lottery numbers while other people's children squirt you with water pistols.

Retirement. I am against it. Stay at home and watch Jerry Springer? How utterly unproductive. Continue producing, you'll have more fun. Besides, the insurance companies embezzled your pension fund anyway.

- Never retire FROM something, always retire TO something
- Now is the time to use your skills to start something you've always wanted to do, something worthwhile
- If you are lazy and not working at eighty, GET A JOB
- In long-lived cultures, retirement is unknown! Everyone produces, some still fathering sprogs at ninety
- Seventy-year-olds know a lot of stuff
- Dream – Plan – Deliver, and I don't mean pizza
- According to the longevity experts, at 65 you are approximately 55% through your genetic potential
- Sitting at home does nothing but provoke feelings of worthlessness (big nocebo), owned up to even by lottery winners, who often face depression or a return to work to do something useful
- Why not work for yourself? You captain, everyone else private. Create! Produce! Serve! Show someone you are still alive. Blink.

Out of Our Minds? Avoid Psychiatry

A pointless life provokes depression. *Mind*, a mental health charity, believes 1 in 4 Brits have a 'mental health problem' at some stage in their lives. By 2020, depression is expected to outstrip heart disease as the leading human health catastrophe, we are told.

'What's the point of it all?' 'Why work?' 'What's it all been about?' 'What the hell will it all matter fifty years from now?' More people are 'mentally ill' today, apparently, than at any other time in history.

Actually, we're not. Mostly, we're victims of lifestyle and circumstance, of what we do to ourselves, the hamster wheel spinning too fast, pathologised into a mental illness by psychiatry and then treated with drugs: Chronic Tax Anxiety Syndrome; Conduct Disorder; Lottery Stress Disorder; Organic Caffeine Mental Disorder; or, if you disagree with your psychiatrist, Denial Disorder. You get the picture.

I am the sworn enemy of a system which stigmatises people with fake mental illnesses, then doses them up. Our schools and retirement homes are full of pharma zombies. My book, *The Mind Game*, dishes the goods on this scoundrel industry and why you need to stay as far away as you can from its clutches. [11] A list of the main 'mental' illnesses is given in *The Mind Game* and *The ABC's of Disease*, which are mostly lifestyle, metabolic or toxin-related problems, which, you'll be delighted to hear, do not have their resolutions in electro-shock or the Prozac bottle.

---

[11] **Day, Phillip,** *The Mind Game*, Credence 2003, www.credence.org

49

It suits psychiatry to tell us we're victims of any one of the frauds in their 'disease' manual, the DSM.[12] Psychiatry is the study of people who don't need to be studied by people who do. A big chunk of the pharmaceutical pie now comes from treating bogus 'mental' conditions. Today, plans are afoot to test every American for 'mental illness'. In Britain, as life speeds out of control on the rodent wheel, we're being taught it's nothing we did, it's merely a chemical imbalance which can be adjusted with drugs.

Yet hyperglycaemia, schizophrenia, depression, behavioural disorders, addictions, anorexia/bulimia, criminal violence, menopausal symptoms, etc. have all been found to have lifestyle/metabolic causations. Can a lifestyle problem provoke a medical problem? Of course. Anger, stress and fear can all stir up physical/mental reactions which can be interpreted as 'illness' (more so if they appear to be chronic). Here's one more entry for the DSM. Medical Testing Disease: If you think you're completely healthy, you've not had enough tests yet.

Thinks
Do you think there is anything wrong with you?

Are you living life too fast, jamming the needles to the red and smoking the rubber to the cord?

When was the last time you took a break?

Is it really *that* bad?

Who can you talk the problem out with?

Avoid Psychiatry.[13]

---

[12] The Diagnostic and Statistical Manual for Mental Disorders

[13] For a full study on psychiatry and its pitfalls, **Day, Phillip** *The Mind Game*, Credence, 2002, www.credence.org

Get Smooching

Love and caring affect us at a deep, physical level, the experts agree (those that pucker up). They are right. Who's loving you? To whom are you giving the keys to your soul and stationwagon? To GET the right person you have to BE the right person, which, broken down, means it's all about values and giving.[14] Plants, animals, humans and even John Prescott have all been found to respond to love. It's a squishy world out there, after all, and one solidly grounded in give and take.

Those hurt by relationships, please take your place at the back of that long line (you might have a mental illness). Do your *values* match your partner's? If they don't, there will be conflict. Values are not the same as goals:

- Do you have friends who vex you?
- Do you share your partner's hopes, goals and values?
- Do you respect each other?
- Can you commit?
- Do you give more than you take?

I'm Outta Here – The Art of Playing

Take four-week holidays! TAKE FOUR-WEEK HOLIDAYS! 𝔗𝔞𝔨𝔢 𝔣𝔬𝔲𝔯-𝔴𝔢𝔢𝔨 𝔥𝔬𝔩𝔦𝔡𝔞𝔶𝔰! *Take four-week holidays!* **Take four-week holidays!**

'One in three British workers fail to take their full annual holiday entitlement, a survey has shown. Instead, they put in 36 million hours of free overtime, giving bosses almost £1 billion in unpaid work every year –'

---

[14] **Buscaglia, Leo** *Love*, Slack Inc., 1972, www.buscaglia.com

And if we do go on holiday –

The survey of nearly 6,000 workers by the Chartered management Institute found nearly half stay in contact with their employer while they are away.' – Daily Mail, 15th June 2005

No! No! No! No! No!

Behavioural patterns are formed over a 15- to 30-day period through repetition and a state of emotional excitement. They break over the same period. Few of us take four-week holidays, which is why we still have bats in the belfry upon our return. Pavlov patterning relies on location, so clearing off somewhere nice geographically to break our stride makes all the sense in the world, especially if we go to *play*. Not for two weeks. Four weeks.

Take those who relax you. Leave the kids at home if necessary (straight-jackets are for this). Go forth and frivolate, you've earned it. The first ten days of your four-week readjustment are usually spent cussing out Spanish waiters and being thoroughly unpleasant to everybody as the mental puke gushes out. After, serenity and bliss will prevail, or your travel agent will give you your money back.

- Now go and play
- Do not take the laptop or anything connected with work
- Do not phone home and get stressed
- Do not phone work
- Lose the mobile phone
- Do not *ever* tell your boss where he can reach you
- Eat real, living, organic whole-foods
- Exercise (more play)

- Behave inappropriately (even more play). It's a holiday
- Dreaming comes easier with a magenta sunset and a Mai-Tai. These are the times of refreshing and cerebral inspiration. Get refreshed, sunshine

Laugh? Easy For You to Say –

Laughter reduces stress. Laughter makes everyone look more appealing (apart from Jack Nicholson). Laughter says, 'See, I can put on a red nose the same as everyone else.' Laughter is actually pretty funny, so you should do it. Often.

- Change your posture to portray confidence and humour
- Plan laughter outings with friends which you know will be a riot, e.g. comedy clubs, a funny film, the barricades at a G8 summit
- Get friends who know how to shake their bellies
- Then tell the Germans and French how to do it

Laughter is the best medicine. You cannot patent it.

Not much laughter in a doctor's surgery.

Money

Is a tool, not an altar. Those who worship money are stressed at the idea of losing it and do not have loftier goals. Saying, 'I wish to be a millionaire' is like saying, 'I wish to have a million oysters'. Oysters are a commodity. What do you want to do with them?

- Do not be dysfunctional around money. It's only money
- Expenditure rises to meet income. Are you living beyond your means?

- Accept money graciously
- Give money graciously
- Use money wisely
- You can't take it with you
- The answer to a money problem is not medication, alcohol or kicking the dog, it's money
- To get out of a money problem you need to increase your income while decreasing your expenses
- Dream – plan – deliver. Stay/get out of debt
- A workman is worthy of his wages. Pay those who work for you a little more than they deserve
- Nobody's last words were ever: 'Darn, I wish I'd spent more time at the office.' (except Ricky Gervais)
- Your bank manager is not losing one wink of sleep over your overdraft, unless you're reading this, Nick Leeson

Make Good Choices

What our lives become is down to the choices we make. A valuable pattern to install is to *practise making conscious choices for the first thirty days on everything*. What you eat, what you wear, what you say, etc. Some people start in just one area and then expand the concept. For instance, every day you have a choice about what to eat. But from a biochemical standpoint, there are no choices. Make the wrong choice with food consistently and nature will sharpen her sword for you.

Make good choices.

If faced with a difficult decision, rephrase the question: What would Napoleon do? What would God do? What would your hero do? I can speak better for them sometimes than I can for myself. Thus I change the focus of a difficult decision and the answer is often before me. I don't procrastinate. Procrastination's linking pain to taking action, a sure sign you're a sissy.

Simplify! Simplify! Simplify!

Most attitude problems, 'mental illness', anger, stress, road rage, toilet-seat rage, etc. derive from the hamster wheel spinning too fast. Some try to hang on for grim death (Whee!!), while others cause the onlookers to duck as they fly off into the water dish. Usually a psychiatrist fishes them out.

Learn More About Yourself
- Are you stressed?
- Are you doing too much?
- Do you have road rage? Hotel rage? Parking rage?
- Do you have free time when you can do nothing?
- What comes out of your mouth?
- Do you surround yourself with noise at every opportunity (TV, radio, parties, computer games, Graham Norton?)
- Try driving around in the car with nothing on (the radio)
- Try switching off the TV
- Exercise 60 – 90 mins a day outside (play)
- Allocate at least an hour each day/evening simply to veg
- Re-acquaint yourself with the names of your children
- Discover your spouse
- Rule your domain
- Be

Thinks
- The body and mind are one. Medicine does not teach this.
- How healthy are your thoughts?
- What you believe and what is important to you guides your actions

- Love and caring affect you at a deep, physical level
- Pain in, pain out. Pleasure in, pleasure out
- Surviving stress is knowing when to walk away
- When was the last time you took a consecutive, four-week holiday?

You Are What You Eat: The Physical

Eat burgers for fifteen years, become a burger. Food can change your mood (especially sugar), Valentine's Day depends on it. Eat living foods to live, dead foods to die. In my books *Health Wars* and *Food for Thought*, I tackle the subject of what works and what doesn't. In *The Mind Game*, I examine the foods that can do you in as well as the ones that will bail you out.

At the end of this chapter is the Food For Thought Lifestyle Regimen. It's a check-list for those wishing to raise the bar of their physical standard if they are already moderately healthy. We'll look at it in a minute. Remember, if you suffer from an ailment, specific dietary changes may be required. *The ABC's of Disease*, our index compendium, covers a whole rash of disease conditions with their associated, recommended dietary changes.

Hypo/Hyperglycaemia

The brain runs on glucose, claiming up to 30% of the body's production of the essential sugar. 'Blood sugar' levels are vital to the correct functioning of both brain and body. When this delicate balancing act is disrupted, hypoglycaemia (low blood sugar) or hyperglycaemia (high blood sugar) may result, throw both the body and mind into turmoil. It is estimated that 1 in 4 of us may suffer from some form of glucose intolerance, resulting in hypo/hyperglycaemia and, eventually, diabetes mellitus, type 2.

Symptoms: Trembling, anxiety, fatigue, wobbly if hungry, confusion, irritability, palpitations, blurred vision, cold hands and feet, low blood pressure, blackouts, angry outbursts, rambling speech, violence, depression, inappropriate or strange behaviour, forgetfulness, road rage, and an inability to concentrate.

Sugar Bombing

Today's penchant for eating truck-loads of high-energy, refined high-glycaemic carbohydrates, such as pastries, bread, pasta, sweets, etc., washed down with sugary drinks or alcoholic beverages, means that a tremendous amount of excess glucose, which isn't being burnt off as fuel (lack of exercise), has to be dealt with somehow. Initially, as much as possible is stored in the liver and body tissues in the form of glycogen. As more sugar is stuffed into our sagging bodies daily, the liver swells like a balloon to accommodate it, waiting in vain for the garbage truck to take it out of the body (detoxification/ elimination).[15] The truck almost never arrives because we do not detoxify our bodies (sugar has also been linked to constipation).[16] Finally, reaching its limit, the liver has had enough and pours the sucrose toxins it has accumulated back into the bloodstream in the form of fatty acids, which are then taken to storage bins in the inactive areas of the body, namely the belly, thighs, hips, breasts and the backs of our upper arms (triceps area).

Once the inactive storage areas are filled to capacity, the body begins distributing the metabolite acids into the active organs, such as the heart and kidneys.[17] These fats accumulate as rapidly as the sucrose continues to pour in, impairing the

---

[15] **Goulart, F S** *American Fitness*, "Are You Sugar Smart?" March-April 1991, pp.34-38

[16] Ibid.

[17] **Yudkin, Kang and Bruckdorfer** "Effects of High Dietary Sugar", *British Journal of Medicine*, #281, 1980, p.1396

functioning of vital organs, causing hormonal imbalance[18], creating lethargy, abnormal blood pressure as the circulatory and lymph systems are invaded, depleting vital vitamin C reserves, threatening the cardiovascular system.[19] An overabundance of white cells occurs, leading to the retardation of tissue formation. The system is nearing collapse at this point, but still the sugar keeps a-coming –

How about the rampant alcoholic consumption, which in itself leads to chaotic blood sugar patterns and diabetes? How about the cellulite, varicose veins and the rotten teeth?[20] [21] How about the kids bouncing off the walls with mineral depletion, ADD and ADHD because sucrose robs minerals, impairs brain function, resulting in increased emotional instability, concentration difficulties, hyperactivity and violence in the classroom,[22] [23] ending up with a Ritalin or Prozac prescription, black eyes from fighting, detention, lousy grades – and even a school shooting or two?[24]

[18] **Yudkin, J** "Metabolic Changes Induced by Sugar in Relation to Coronary Heart Disease and Diabetes", *Nutrition and Health*, Vol.5, #1-2, 1987: pp.5-8

[19] **Pamplona, Bellmunt, Portero and Prat** "Mechanisms of Glycation in Atherogenesis", *Medical Hypotheses*, #40, 1990, pp.174-181

[20] **Cleave and Campbell** *Diabetes, Coronary Thrombosis and the Saccharine Disease*, John Wright and Sons, Bristol, UK: 1960

[21] **Glinsman, Irausquin and Youngmee** "Evaluation of Health Aspects of Sugars Contained in Carbohydrate Sweeteners", Report from FDA's Sugar Task Force, Center for Food Safety and Applied Nutrition, Washington DC: 1986, p.39

[22] **Schauss, Alexander** *Diet, Crime and Delinquency*, Parker House, Berkeley, CA: 1981

[23] **Goldman, J et al** "Behavioural Effects of Sucrose on Preschool Children", *Journal of Abnormal Child Psychology*, #14, 1986, pp.565-577

[24] *Journal of Abnormal Psychology*, #85, 1985

Getting it Sorted

Now, did you know **when** you eat can be every bit as important as **what** you eat? Welcome to the Science of Natural Hygiene:

The Body's Natural Digestive Cycles

Natural Hygiene teaches that the human body's digestive system goes through three eight-hour cycles every twenty-four hours:

Noon – 8pm: **Appropriation** of food (eating and digestion)
8pm – 4am: **Assimilation** of food (absorption and use)
4am – Noon: **Elimination** (excretion of waste products)

It is not hard to see these cycles in action. It is also uncomfortably clear when these cycles are thrown into turmoil, for example, when we eat a pizza late at night or gargle down the 'farm-fresh' breakfast. Let's briefly review:

APPROPRIATION (12 Noon – 8pm)

A clock-adjusted body prefers the Appropriation Cycle to commence at noon. Notice most can actually make it through to twelve without the heart-on-a-plate breakfast since morning hours are spent by the body in Elimination (see below). Once past noon, however, we become uncomfortable if we do not eat. Our body craves nourishment during Appropriation and will let us know of its needs in no uncertain terms if we are remiss in supplying the necessary fodder. The most important rule during Appropriation is *to eat only when your body is hungry.*

ASSIMILATION (8pm – 4am)

Assimilation (nutrient extraction and use) occurs mostly during sleeping hours, which makes all the sense in the world when we are resting and the digestive system can crank up and do its thing

60

without interruption. Night-time is naturally not a good time for Appropriation (eating and digestion) because of the horizontal angles involved. During Assimilation, the body extracts nutrients in our intestines, which are twelve times the length of our trunks, designed as they are to keep high-water-content, unrefined plant dietary food in their clutches until all the nutrients are withdrawn.

If you leave three hours between your last meal and when you go to bed, a properly combined supper, along the lines explained, will have already left the stomach and be on its peaceful way down the Channel Tunnel for squeezing and extracting by the time you lay your precious head on the pillow. During the night, your body is putting all those nutrients to work replenishing your systems, replacing damaged cells and allowing the blood and lymph systems to gather waste and take it to the excretory points for collection.

ELIMINATION (4am – 12 Noon)
At 4am, Elimination cuts in and the garbage truck arrives to take out the junk. Your body has sorted through the food it has processed, and rejected what cannot be absorbed and satisfactorily metabolised into its constituent nutrients for further use. Elimination is simply the removal of waste matter from the body, be it fibrous, non-metabolised food, toxins or waste products the body generates. These are shunted out via the underarm, bowel, bladder, glands, etc. Emergency elimination can be dramatic when time is of the essence in getting rid of dangerously toxic material before the body's internal organs are threatened. Examples of this are diarrhoea, a waterfall of a nose during colds, and of course, vomiting. Or my favourite, which can be seen outside The Pig and Whistle Pub in London on a Friday midnight – projectile vomiting.

Elimination is the most thwarted digestive cycle of the three - an abuse that has led to chronic obesity in our populations and catastrophic ill-health. *Elimination is always sabotaged by large, badly combined breakfasts, the processing of which prevents the daily elimination function of getting rid of waste.* Thus the junk stays put and gets filed in the parts of our bodies where it can do the least harm (slow turn-over tissues such as fats). We look at our naked bodies in the mirror with horror: *"Good grief, my bum DOES look big in this. I look like a beached whale."* Your body is naturally offended at the insult being aimed in its direction and replies: *"Then unplug me, Einstein, and let's get rid of the whale –"*

Let food be your medicine and medicine be your food

Dump the big breakfast and graze *sparingly* on fruit before noon on an empty stomach. This assists the Elimination Cycle in completing its job (shedding fat too!). The fructose will raise blood sugar and turn off your hunger switch. Commence eating meals from noon, ensuring 80% of what you eat comes out of a kitchen garden, as much as possible eaten raw. Natural Hygiene is about keeping the body in balance nutritionally, metabolically, and replenished with water. 70% of our planet's surface is water, our bodies are 70% water, so it makes sense to eat a diet consisting of at least 70 - 80% high-water-content, high-fibre, living, whole, organic foods which have not had water and the accompanying nutrients stripped out.[25] Speaking of which –

---

[25] For more information on Natural Hygiene, see *Food For Thought* or *Health Wars*

Water, Water and Not a Drop to Drink

Perhaps the most overlooked problem in the western cultures is chronic dehydration. Many of today's designer drinks are diuretic in their effect (water-expelling) because their acidic compositions require the body to surrender water to eliminate their harmful residues. Sodas are especially harmful in that they require large amounts of body-water to neutralise the phosphoric acid component (2.8 pH). Cells that started off healthy and 'plum-like' shrivel to prunes as water, the stuff of life, is progressively egressed. The sick in our hospitals are fed the sodas, tea and coffee they ask for in woeful ignorance of the damage wrought to their micro cell-world within.

There is no more important substance for good health than water. Your body cries out for it, your blood is made up of it, nerves, heart, lungs, bowels and brain do not function without it, yet we answer the body's thirst signals with tea, coffee, Fanta, Diet Coke, Budweiser and drugs! Hardly any wonder most western nations have a pub/bar culture to deal with the ravening thirst of their citizens.

Many illnesses respond well to adequate hydration, according to world-renowned water expert, Dr Fereydoon Batmanghelidj, especially *brain function*. The brain comprises 2% of the body's total weight, yet receives 15-20% of the blood supply, mostly comprised of water. Dehydration will affect cognitive ability drastically, and, through histamine's action, can create depressive states (many anti-depressants are anti-histamines). However, with a daily clean water intake, mental performance is enhanced, limbs operate, blood thinned, pain banished, bowels happy, skin lustrous and clear, toxins flushed away. My booklet, *Water: The Stuff of Life*, will fill you in.[26]

Don't drink tap water, filter it! The best filtration system for the money, in my view, is reverse osmosis. There are more expensive filters if you can spring for them, but for a stable, clean and cheap source of water conveniently at your tap, with chlorine, hormones, fluoride, etc. removed, RO gets my vote. May I also wholeheartedly recommend every thirst-wracked body read Dr Batmanghelidj's glorious *Water and Salt* book.[27] Dr Batman is right to anticipate his findings will open the sluice gates of a new understanding in medical science. Which, if one pauses to ponder, may be the ultimate irony. Two atoms of hydrogen and one of oxygen. Set to flood the world with its substance.

Again.

---

[26] **Day, Phillip** *Water – The Stuff of Life*, Credence 2004. RO filtration units are available through www.credence.org

[27] **Batmanghelidj, F** *Water and Salt, Your Healers From Within*, Tagman Press, 2005, www.credence.org

The Food for Thought Lifestyle Regimen

For OK bodies wanting to be healthier. Banish bad habits. See how your current regime compares with the following:

➢ Eat a little or no meat in the diet. Meat should not comprise more than 10% of the diet. Meat consumed should be hormone- and pesticide-free. White meat is better than red. Avoid pork and all porky things (bacon, prosciutto, hot-dogs, ham, salami, yadda, yadda)

➢ Avoid sugar, dairy, coffee and alcohol

➢ Eat properly constituted, high water-content, high-fibre, living, whole, organic foods, **a high percentage consumed raw**. If you want hot, briefly steam your veggies, do not murder them. Remember, heat kills enzymes over 45°C (118°F). Excellent recipes are provided in *Food For Thought*

➢ The ideal balance is: 80%/20% alkali/acid foods. Most diets today comprise 90% acid/10% alkali. Ensure 80% of your food comes out of a kitchen garden (fruits, vegetables, pulses, legumes, haricots, etc.). Juice greens. We have an excellent juicing book [28]

➢ Broiled fish, deep and cold caught, eaten sparingly is OK

➢ Hydrate the body (2 litres (4 pints) of clean, fresh water a day). Reverse osmosis filtration, bang for the buck, is best

---

[28] **Constantino, Maria** *The Book of Energy Drinks*, www.credence.org

65

- Dump the breakfast, which is eaten during your elimination cycle. Instead, consume fruit before noon on an empty stomach *sparingly*. Prefer fruits with a low sugar-conversion, such as apples and pears
- Eat *small* meals, ensuring a) you don't go hungry, and b) the body has a constant supply of nutrients
- **Take a basic supplement program** consisting of ionised colloidal trace minerals, antioxidant tablets, Vit C and B complexes and essential fats
- Exercise to get everything moving. This assists in detoxing the body (lymph, etc.) in an oxygen-rich environment. 60 – 90 minutes a day in the open air. If exercise = pain, play instead
- Rest. Rest. Rest. Rest. Rest
- Reduce environmental toxicity (avoid jobs handling dangerous chemicals, radiation, blood, alien molecular acid, etc.)
- Use safe personal care products
- Use safe household products[29]

AVOID:

- Pork products (bacon, sausage, hot-dogs, luncheon meat, ham, etc.) These are high in nitrites and are homotoxins which can cause high blood urea and dikitopiprazines, which cause brain tumours and leukaemia.[30]
- Scavenger meats (inc. ALL shellfish and other carrion-eaters). Carrion-eaters, pork and shellfish in particular, concentrate toxins in their tissues, which we consume

---

[29] Neways International, www.neways.com

[30] Day, Phillip, *Food for Thought*, op. cit; *Biologic Therapy*, "Adverse influence of pork consumption on human health", Vol. 1, No. 2, 1983

to our detriment. The same goes for the elimination organs of commercially raised animals, such as liver and kidney, which can be high in drug and pesticide residues

➢ Aspartame/saccharin, artificial sweeteners. These are known mental impairment problems and cancer risks

➢ Refined sugar/flour/rice. SUCROSE FEEDS CANCER and other sugar-sensitive illnesses (arthritis, diabetes, yeast and fungal problems, etc.). Restricted amounts of wholegrain bread are OK. Drastically reduce consumption of grains. Use only wholegrain rice. Consume no sugars other than those contained naturally in whole foods

➢ Hydrogenated & partially hydrogenated fats (margarine)

➢ Junk (processed) food, including fizzy sodas and other soft drinks containing sugar, additives, artificial sweeteners or phosphoric acid, drunk out of aluminium cans

➢ Fat-free foods. Essential fats are *essential!*

➢ Olestra, canola, soy, etc. Avoid fake or synthetic fats. Soy, in its unfermented state (meat and milk substitute products), disrupts the hormone (endocrine) system, blocks the absorption of calcium and magnesium, and acts like estrogen in the body.[31] Small amounts of fermented soy products (soy sauce and miso) are OK

➢ Polluted water (chlorinated or fluoridated – see *Health Wars*, 'Water Under the Bridge')

➢ Caffeine products

---

[31] See **The Shadow of Soy** by Sean McNary Carson: *Food for Thought*, Credence Publications 2004. Also, www.soyonlineservice.co.nz

- ➢ Alcohol products
- ➢ Excess refined salt. Better to spice food with whole salt (sea/Celtic) or ground kelp to maintain a healthy iodine intake

Chemical Alley

Detox your manor. Home and the workplace play host to a veritable witch's brew of dodgy chemicals we happily use without a by-your-leave because we assume they have been pronounced safe. THIS IS NOT THE CASE! The chemical industry is largely self-regulating (naturally).

Shampoos, toothpastes, make-up, anti-perspirants, face creams, etc. variously purchased from supermarkets or respectable stores can contain carcinogens such as the ethanolamines (MEA, DEA, TEA, etc) and other gruesome gunk. I have a special section dedicated to this subject in *The ABC's of Disease, Health Wars, Cancer: Why We're Still Dying to Know the Truth* and *The Mind Game*. The best company to consult for non-toxic, high-quality replacements is Neways International, now in over forty countries around the planet. No, we're not commercially affiliated. Find a distributor near you and they'll explain the problem and solution. **DON'T POISON YOURSELF!**

Summary

All right, let's review and then we're out of here:

1. Obtain control over your sense of certainty. Know why you do what you do, and why things are the way they are
2. Live one day at a time
3. Own a good conscience
4. Be an overcomer
5. Create a positive outlook and optimism for the future. Set goals. Know where you are going every day
6. Create enjoyable wholesome, optimistic experiences every day
7. Guard input. Switch off the TV/radio, especially the news, and see how you feel. None of it usually affects you directly and the rest is the weather (which they always lie about)
8. Think good thoughts. Do not entertain impromptu, evil imaginings. You can't stop the birds flying over your head, but you can stop 'em nesting in your hair
9. Make good choices. Put 'Post It' notes with these three words on all your food cabinets for the first thirty days to force conscious decisions on what to eat until your new patterns are formed
10. Relationships: Restructure the friendship arena. Do you have friends who drag you down?

11. Take frequent holidays to erase brain-patterning. Four weeks in the absence of those who cause you stress and worry. Different geographical location.
12. Worry/stress situations: how are you processing them?
13. Reconcile your fear of death. Get a belief system which gives you context and explains why you're here
14. You are what you eat: Change to the Food for Thought Lifestyle Regimen. If you are sick, learn about your illness and decide on an appropriate action. *The ABC's of Disease* covers most ailments. Let your treatment be *your* decision
15. Keep your exposure to doctors and psychiatrists to a minimum
16. Embark on a basic supplement program of vitamins, minerals and essential fats
17. Detoxify body, mind and environment
18. Simplify! Simplify! Simplify! Create empty time
19. Lose the mobile phone
20. Get out of debt
21. Live in the present
22. Listen to what comes out of your mouth. It's a good indication of when you need that four-week holiday
23. Forgive
24. Create
25. Serve
26. And keep doing all of the above until your need for oxygen ceases

So Finally –

Who's for a good life? Who's willing to help themselves and others mount the halcyon pinnacle? What more important mission can there be than emotional freedom, loss of worry, goals met, a life well lived, minefields avoided? There's a beautiful world out there to savour and explore to your heart's fullest content. Are you up for adventure?

Fret not, want not, play and proliferate. Flog the hamster wheel on eBay. Farm Christmas trees in Montana. Help those less fortunate. Live each day to the full. And know why you're doing it.

In the meantime, I am certain the powers that run everything are gradually sorting themselves out in the Great Beyond. I sometimes hear voices:

'God is dead!' - Nietsche
'Nietsche is dead!' - God

Other Disorders
(where to go for more information)

THE ABC'S OF DISEASE is Credence's index compendium on over eighty disorders, what they are, what the symptoms are, and what can be done about them nutritionally, according to experts. For more information on specific disorders:

Chicken pox, opportunistic (infectious) diseases, influenza (flu), malaria, measles, mumps, rubella, severe acute respiratory syndrome (SARS), smallpox, tuberculosis, typhoid, etc.
**See: *Wake up to Health in the 21st Century*
by Steven Ransom**

Cancers: brain, bowel, breast, cervical, liver, lung, osteo, ovarian, pancreatic, prostate, skin, etc.
**See: *Cancer: Why We're Still Dying to Know the Truth*
by Phillip Day
Also: *Great News on Cancer in the 21st Century*
by Steven Ransom**

Bad breath, constipation, diarrhoea, esophageal reflux, heart diseases, high blood pressure, lactose intolerance, poisonings, putrefaction and misc. digestion problems
**See: *Health Wars*
by Phillip Day**

ADD/ADHD, agitation, amnesia, anorexia nervosa, antisocial behaviour, autism, bedwetting, bulimia, chemical imbalances, convulsions, criminal behaviour, depression, drug addiction, dyslexia, epilepsy, facial swelling, glucose intolerance, hallucinations, hirsutism, histadelia, histapenia, hyperactivity, hypersexuality, infantile colic, irritability, leaky gut syndrome, nerve pain, nightmares, phobias, schizophrenia, seizures, smoking addiction, stress, suicidal tendencies, twitches

See: *The Mind Game*
by Phillip Day

Acquired Immuno-Deficiency Syndrome and related disorders
See: The Truth About HIV
By Steven Ransom and Phillip Day

These titles and more are available through Credence's website at:

www.credence.org

Contacts! Contacts! Contacts!

If you wish to purchase more copies of this booklet or obtain any of Credence's other book and tape products, please use the contact details below. Credence has local sales offices in a number of countries. Please see our website at **www.credence.org** for further details:

> **UK Orders:** (01622) 832386
> **UK Fax:** (01622) 833314
> **www.credence.org**
> **e-mail:** sales@credence.org

Obtaining Health Products

If you need more information or help with any of the materials discussed in this book, please use the above contact details. Alternatively, you may contact us at:

Credence Publications
PO Box 3
TONBRIDGE
Kent TN12 9ZY
England
infopack@credence.org

The Campaign for Truth in Medicine

WHAT IS CTM?

The Campaign for Truth in Medicine is a worldwide organisation dedicated to educating the public on health issues and pressing for change in areas of science and medicine where entrenched scientific error, ignorance and vested interests are costing lives. Our ranks comprise doctors, scientists, researchers, biochemists, politicians, industry executives and

members of the public, all of who have come to recognise that in key areas of disease, drug treatments and healthcare philosophy, the medical, chemical and political establishments are pursuing the wrong course with the maximum of precision, even when their own scientific research has warned of the dangers of pursuing these courses.

CTM STANDS FOR CHOICE IN HEALTHCARE

Millions today use nutritional supplements and alternative health strategies for themselves and their families, and yet, increasingly, the public's freedom to choose is being eroded by government legislation and attempts by the pharmaceutical conglomerates to 'buy out' the alternative health market. CTM stands for the people's right to choose the healthcare system they feel is right for them, free of big business interference, pointless government regulation, and coercion by the medical establishment which often attempts to compel its own dubious remedies upon an unwilling public.

CTM STANDS FOR SPREADING THE GOOD NEWS

Every month, CTM sends out EClub, its global online magazine, to keep subscribers informed of the latest news, developments, scandals and great news in healthcare and other relevant issues. Within EClub, doctors, researchers, journalists, scientists and leading healthcare advocates share their tips, views and strategies with hundreds of thousands around the world. EClub represents the news you are not being told; information that can literally change and save lives. Don't miss out on this vital resource, forwarded FREE to you every month! To join, please visit www.campaignfortruth.com and click on the 'Join' tab.

Be part of a different future. One that celebrates life!

HOW TO ORDER CREDENCE PRODUCTS

Credence has offices and distributors in many countries around the world. If you would like more information, or wish to purchase any of the Credence titles described, please use the details in the **Contacts!** section of this book. Alternatively, why not visit Credence's comprehensive web-site at **www.credence.org**, which contains secure on-line global stores, a fully searchable database, our famous testimonies section, and many other great features.

Please note: Items not available in your regional shop may be obtained through our default 'Rest of World' store.

About the Author

Phillip Day was born in England in 1960. He was educated at Selwyn and Charterhouse, and throughout his twenties had a successful entrepreneurial career founding businesses in sales and marketing. With a firm grounding in the ways of the media, Phillip's research career began after he became interested in wars going on in the realms of health and politics over issues that were being deliberately withheld or misreported to the public.

Phillip Day heads up the publishing and research organisation Credence, now located in many countries around the world, which collates the work provided by researchers in many fields. Credence's intention is to work with the establishments and organisations concerned to resolve issues that are harming the public, and to provide the necessary information for citizens to make their own informed choices in these vital matters. Phillip's speaking schedule takes him to audiences all over the world.

Phillip Day is married to Samantha and lives in Kent, England.